21st Century
Basic Skills
Library

KIDS CAN MAKE MANNERS COUNT
TAKING TURNS!

3

by Katie Marsico

Cherry Lake Publishing • Ann Arbor, Michigan

Published in the United States of America
by Cherry Lake Publishing
Ann Arbor, Michigan
www.cherrylakepublishing.com

Content Adviser: Tonia Bock, PhD, Associate Professor of Psychology,
St. Thomas University, St. Paul, Minnesota

Photo Credits: All photos ©Keri Langlois, except page 12, ©Rob Marmion/
Shutterstock, Inc.

Library of Congress Cataloging-in-Publication Data
Marsico, Katie, 1980–
  Taking turns / by Katie Marsico.
    p. cm.— (21st century basic skills library) (Kids can make
manners count)
  Includes bibliographical references and index.
  ISBN 978-1-61080-432-5 (lib. bdg.) — ISBN 978-1-61080-519-3 (e-book) —
ISBN 978-1-61080-606-0 (pbk.)
1. Sharing—Juvenile literature. 2. Fairness—Juvenile literature.
3. Courtesy—Juvenile literature. I. Title.
  BJ1533.G4M37 2013
  395.1'22—dc23   2012001515

Cherry Lake Publishing would like to acknowledge
the work of The Partnership for 21st Century Skills.
Please visit www.21stcenturyskills.org for more information.

Printed in the United States of America
Corporate Graphics Inc.
July 2012
CLFA11

TABLE OF CONTENTS

A Puppy Problem

Mia and her brother, Sam, were excited. They had a new puppy!

They raced home after school. Each wanted to walk the puppy.

Mia grabbed the leash first.

Mia liked winning the race and walking their puppy.

Sam was angry. He never got a chance!

He and Mia started fighting all the time.

Making Manners Work

Mia loved Sam.

Yet she did not want to lose the race. That meant losing time with the puppy.

Luckily their mother said she had a **solution**.

Mia and Sam listened to their mom. She talked about being **fair** and taking turns.

Taking turns is one example of having good **manners**.

Their mom pointed out that they had taken turns before.

Mia and her friends took turns on the playground slide.

She and Sam took turns speaking in class by raising their hands.

First Mia, Then Sam

Their mother **suggested** other ways to take turns.

She said they should make a **schedule** for walking the puppy.

Mia would walk the puppy on Sundays, Tuesdays, and Thursdays.

Sam would take his turn on Mondays, Wednesdays, and Fridays.

Mia and Sam walked the puppy together on Saturdays.

Mia held the leash part of the time.

Then Sam took a turn holding it.

Mia and Sam started getting along better.

They stopped fighting over the puppy.

Each of them finally got to spend time with the puppy!

21

Find Out More

BOOK

Chancellor, Deborah. *Good Manners*. New York: Crabtree
   Publishing Company, 2010.

WEB SITE

**U.S. Department of Health and Human Services—
Building Blocks: Manners Quiz**
*www.bblocks.samhsa.gov/family/activities/quizzes/manners.
aspx*
Take a fun online quiz to test how much you know about
manners!

Glossary

fair (FAYR) following rules and not cheating

manners (MA-nurz) behavior that is kind and polite

schedule (SKEJ-ool) a plan for doing something at a certain date
and time

solution (suh-LOO-shuhn) an answer to a problem

suggested (sug-JEST-id) advised or offered ideas

Home and School Connection

Use this list of words from the book to help your child become a better reader. Word games and writing activities can help beginning readers reinforce literacy skills.

a	finally	it	on	slide	to
about	first	leash	one	solution	together
after	for	liked	other	speaking	took
all	Fridays	listened	out	spend	Tuesdays
along	Friends	lose	over	started	turn
and	getting	losing	part	stopped	turns
angry	good	loved	playground	suggested	walk
before	got	luckily	pointed	Sundays	walked
being	grabbed	make	problem	take	walking
better	had	making	puppy	taken	want
brother	having	manners	race	taking	wanted
by	hands	meant	raced	talked	was
chance	he	Mia	raising	that	ways
class	held	mom	said	the	Wednesdays
did	her	Mondays	Sam	their	were
each	his	mother	Saturdays	them	winning
example	holding	never	schedule	then	with
excited	home	new	school	they	work
fair	in	not	she	Thursdays	would
fighting	is	of	should	time	yet

Index

About the Author

Katie Marsico is an author of children's and young-adult reference books. She lives outside of Chicago, Illinois, with her husband and children.